ABRAHAM LINCOLN GOES TO THE THEATRE

Larry Tremblay

Translated by
Chantal Bilodeau

Talonbooks

Talonbooks
P.O. Box 2076, Vancouver, British Columbia, Canada V6B 3S3
www.talonbooks.com

Typeset in Sabon and printed and bound in Canada.
Printed on 100% post-consumer recycled paper.

First printing: 2010

The publisher gratefully acknowledges the financial support of the Canada
Council for the Arts; the Government of Canada through the Book Publishing Industry Development Program; and the Province of British Columbia
through the British Columbia Arts Council and the Book Publishing Tax
Credit for our publishing activities.

Abraham Lincoln va au théâtre by Larry Tremblay was first published in
French in 2008 by Lansman Éditeur. We acknowledge the financial support of
the Government of Canada through the National Translation Program for
Book Publishing, for our translation activities.

Library and Archives Canada Cataloguing in Publication

Tremblay, Larry, 1954–
[Abraham Lincoln va au théâtre. English]
  Abraham Lincoln goes to the theatre / Larry Tremblay ; translated by
Chantal Bilodeau.

Translation of: Abraham Lincoln va au théâtre.
A play.
ISBN 978-0-88922-649-4

  I. Bilodeau, Chantal, 1968– II. Title. III.Title: Abraham Lincoln va
au théâtre. English.

PS8589.R445A6313 2010   C842'.54
C2010-902275-0

In memory of Jean-Louis Millette
wherever you are

Abraham Lincoln va au théâtre premiered in Montreal on April 22, 2008 at l'Espace Go in a Théâtre PàP production with the following cast and crew:

LAUREL:	Maxim Gaudette
HARDY:	Patrice Dubois
ABRAHAM LINCOLN:	Benoît Gouin

With the participation of Étienne Cousineau, Guillaume Cyr and Sacha Samar.

Director:	Claude Poissant
Set Design:	Jean Bard
Costume Design:	Marc Sénécal
Lighting Design:	Martin Labrecque
Original Music:	Nicolas Basque
Movement:	Caroline Laurin-Beaucage
Make-up Design:	Florence Cornet
Assistant Director:	Stéphanie Capistran-Lalonde
Stage Manager:	Stéphanie Capistran-Lalonde
Technical Director:	Alexandre Brunet
Production Manager:	Catherine La Frenière
Directing Intern:	Alexia Bürger

The English-language premiere of *Abraham Lincoln Goes to the Theatre* took place on February 12, 2010 at the 24th Annual Enbridge playRites Festival of New Canadian Plays at Alberta Theatre Projects, Calgary, with the following cast and crew:

LAUREL:	Chris Bullough
HARDY:	Geoffrey Pounsett
ABRAHAM LINCOLN:	Allan Morgan

Director:	Bob White
Set Design:	Scott Reid
Costume Design:	Jenifer Darbellay
Lighting Design:	David Fraser
Sound Design:	Matthew Waddell
Make-up Design:	Whitney Huget-Penner
Production Dramaturg:	Amy Lynn Strilchuk
Production Stage Manager:	Dianne Goodman
Stage Manager:	Marcie Januska
Assistant Stage Manager:	Heather Rycraft
Rehearsal Assistant Stage Manager:	Kelsey Ter Kuile

This translation was commissioned by and developed at the Lark Play Development Center, New York City, with funds from the New York State Council on the Arts and the Canada Council for the Arts.

The playwright and translator acknowledge the assistance of the 2009 Banff Playwrights Colony—a partnership between the Canada Council for the Arts, The Banff Centre and Alberta Theatre Projects.

*The real tragedy is that there is
no devil to buy your soul.*

—Romain Gary

CHARACTERS

An actor dressed like LAUREL

An actor dressed like HARDY

An actor dressed like a wax figure of ABRAHAM LINCOLN

LAUREL

He said: "I'm going to demand the impossible." I didn't
believe him. At least not at first. He probably meant: "It
won't be easy. You'll often be sorry you started on this
journey."

HARDY

He said: "You're going to hate me, cry it's unfair. After
work, you'll have only one desire: To go to sleep to
forget what a monster I am."

LAUREL

I can tell you one thing: After work, the three of us
going for a drink never crossed our minds.

HARDY

With him, there was nothing but work. I don't
remember ever asking how he felt about terrorism,
non-alcoholic beer, the fate of small nations—

LAUREL

—where he had learned his profession, if a school, a
master or a book had been important for him. Or even
a film, an event. It was all very …

HARDY

Very …

LAUREL

We couldn't …

HARDY
 We couldn't love a man like him.

LAUREL
 I never touched him.

HARDY
 Why would you have touched him? Don't mention that
 kind of detail.

LAUREL
 A detail? Not at all. I don't know if his hands were dry
 or sweaty.

HARDY
 So?

LAUREL
 It's important. For me. That kind of detail.

HARDY
 Keep going.

LAUREL
 He had mastered the art of distance. Not for
 superiority. More as a tool.

HARDY
 For perspective, too. You have to get distance to aim
 accurately.

LAUREL
 At the first rehearsal, without saying hello, he opened a
 notebook. For ... fifteen minutes?

HARDY
 At least.

LAUREL

For fifteen minutes, he read to us. We didn't understand a word, right?

HARDY

He was reading very fast. It was about the United States. The Civil War. Confederates, Yankees, slavery, Colonel So and So, General So and So, Abraham Lincoln, the lost children of America, the tragic destiny of America—

LAUREL

Yes, but we didn't understand a word. Slam! He closed the notebook.

HARDY

Silence.

LAUREL

An incredible silence. It was coming from him.

HARDY

Yes, the silence was coming from him. Not from us.

LAUREL

Not from us. No. He had also mastered the art of silence—

HARDY

—and had the power to completely ignore you—

LAUREL

—only to discover you a second later as if he were giving birth to you.

HARDY

He had the gift of terror like others have the gift of healing.

LAUREL
  I wanted to be him.

HARDY
  Don't say that.

LAUREL
  Why not?

HARDY
  You're annoying.

LAUREL
  Keep going.

HARDY
  I'm too good to you.

LAUREL
  Thank you. Keep going.

HARDY
  Slam! He closed the notebook. Then silence. A long
  silence. How long?

LAUREL
  Ten minutes.

HARDY
  At least. He's standing. Like this.

LAUREL
  Yes, like that. His legs spread in a strange way. Then he
  shouts:

LAUREL & HARDY
  "What's this smell? Don't play dumb, I'm talking about
  you two! Turn around! Turn back! You've looked
  around, you can see the extent of the damages. No?

Yes? Don't both answer at the same time. So? What's this smell? Can't you smell what you two little persons are fabricating on the sly? Mean, ugly little persons. The smell of holiness, is that it?"

LAUREL

I thought: Yes, that's it. The smell of holiness. We're two actors. We want to be the best. To escape dying of banality, we insist on being martyrs. We want people to gouge our eyes out with a spoon. To break our fingers with a nutcracker. To rip our skin with a cheese grater. To put on display, in the centre courts of large shopping malls, our greyish remains which exude an aroma of rose, lavender or pine depending on the season and the region.

HARDY

Don't exaggerate.

LAUREL

That's what I thought.

HARDY

You've got a screw loose.

LAUREL

You don't agree?

HARDY

That's not the point.

LAUREL

Do you know any actor who doesn't want to be the best of his time? Do you? We're all willing to be martyrs to achieve—

HARDY

OK. Fine. Let's keep going.

LAUREL & HARDY
"The smell of holiness. That's it, right? Two actors
willing to do anything for an experience! Willing to
dive into an abyss of stupidity or plainly assassinate
their progenitor. Am I right? Willing to castrate
themselves if the play requires it. If I require it. Right,
you puny half-witted mutts with droopy eyes? Ah! Do
you know why I chose you out of thirty of your peers?
Yes? No? Not a clue? Not even the faintest idea?"

LAUREL
No. Why us? No. I don't know. Yes, why the two of us?
Yes, why did we agree to audition with thirty of our
peers, all extraordinary actors—generous, open like
shells under the sun? Why are we the ones who got
chosen? Us. No, I don't know. We're the best, perhaps.
That's what I might have thought. But if I thought that,
I thought it very quickly and, for sure, I didn't say it out
loud. Just thought it quickly enough to think I had
never thought it.

LAUREL & HARDY
"Take a look at yourselves! Ridiculous! And by that I
mean: You make a grotesque duo. The mere sight of
you makes us want to hit you and rejoice in not being
you. You're so human, so open. A trash heap of
humanity. You were the perfect actors."

LAUREL
He grabbed you. He said: "You, the fat one ..."

HARDY
Yes.

LAUREL & HARDY
"I will call you Hardy."

HARDY
And to you, he said: "You, the skinny one!"

LAUREL
Yes.

LAUREL & HARDY
"I will call you Laurel. Laurel and Hardy. Understand? Now make me laugh. Entertain me. Think of it as a warm-up exercise."

HARDY
That, as it turns out, wasn't easy.

LAUREL
The warm-up exercise. To entertain. No, hard. Very hard to make someone laugh. Right?

HARDY
You made faces. Show us. Show us how you made the faces.

LAUREL
Like this. And like this. And this one too. You too, you tried to make faces. But it was lame. Lame as shit. Really lame.

HARDY
OK, we get it.

LAUREL
Show us how painfully lame your faces were. Come on!

HARDY
What do you want? Huh? What do you want? To prove you have a Ph.D. in making faces? Is that what you want?

LAUREL
Touchy.

HARDY
I can fart at will. You want to hear?

Silence.

LAUREL
Well?

HARDY
Well?

LAUREL & HARDY
"Well? Lame. You're definitely ready for TV. Lame. To be put under contract as soon as possible. Practise making me laugh. I'll be back in ten minutes. I'm going to get a sandwich. When I get back, be divine."

HARDY
He came back an hour later.

LAUREL
An hour spent making faces.

HARDY
Speak for yourself.

LAUREL
I am speaking for myself.

HARDY
It was obvious he had eaten more than a sandwich.

LAUREL
Very obvious. He has a small packet in his hand which I first take for a sugar packet. He delicately tears it and extracts a paper square. It smells like citronella. He

carefully unfolds the paper and wipes his hands with it, finger by finger, extremely slowly. It's magnificent. I'm captivated. I want to applaud him. Want to kiss his fingers. Never in my life have I seen someone wipe his fingers with so much precision and mystery.

HARDY
Don't say that. It's disgusting.

LAUREL
I'm being honest.

HARDY
That kind of honesty we can do without.

LAUREL
He comes toward me. I make a face. To make him laugh. Because that's what he asked me to do. He looks me in the eye. It gives me goose bumps. And I'm not just playing with words. When I say "goose bumps," I'm talking about a goose and bumps, nothing else.

HARDY
You're right, you look like a goose. A featherless goose being washed in a sink before going into the oven.

LAUREL
Silence. Another one of his damned silences which he throws in our faces like a wet towel. He says to me:

LAUREL & HARDY
"Fear makes people smell bad. You smell ... bad."

LAUREL
Then he spoke to you. He said:

LAUREL & HARDY
"You too, you smell ... bad. It's good. It's very good."

HARDY
We couldn't understand what he was trying to tell us.
He raised his arm and made a fist.

LAUREL
For five minutes—five minutes, I'm not exaggerating—
he tensed his arm. Like this. I started to cry.

HARDY
Eventually, he had to let go.

LAUREL
I was ashamed of my tears. I felt feminine. No.
Childish.

HARDY
You've always been a tears-on-demand actor. At every
line, your eyes are about to drown. You confuse your
character's truth with the weakness of your own nature.
You've played with your feelings too much. You're just
a pile of emotions, a shed, a warehouse, a public
square, everyone's brothel. That's what you were telling
yourself behind your tears.

LAUREL
I was also telling myself: Why not do the impossible?
When you think of it, that's what we always demand
from actors.

[2]

HARDY
My name is Leonard Brannigan. I'm married. I have
two kids. A six-year-old daughter, Sandra. And a two-
year-old, Lea. Sandra and Lea—two little girls we

adopted, my wife and I. We brought them back from
Brazil. They're our joy. A real and simple joy. You?

LAUREL
Me. Nothing.

HARDY
Talk about yourself.

LAUREL
I don't want to.

HARDY
Introduce yourself.

LAUREL
My name is Chris. Chris Levine.

HARDY
Add something.

LAUREL
What?

HARDY
I don't know. Decide.

LAUREL
I live alone. It's sad. You never get used to it. I believe in
the idea of a soul mate. I prefer to believe in it. Yes, I
prefer to believe that somewhere in the world, there's
someone just for me.

HARDY
Go get it.

LAUREL
You're married. I envy married people. How peaceful it
must be. I'm always on the lookout. I have heartburn. I

don't vote. I don't believe in politics anymore. I like
animals. I like a job well done.

HARDY
What are you trying to prove? Go get it.

LAUREL
My favourite actor is Al Pacino. When I saw him in
Dog Day Afternoon, I decided I would be an actor too.
In school, I was reserved. Shy even. I started doing
theatre to overcome my shyness.

HARDY
Listen, you could talk for hours, it wouldn't change
what people think of you.

LAUREL
You go get it!

HARDY
OK.

LAUREL
You were shy too. You told me.

HARDY
OK, everybody gets it. We're neurotic actors.

LAUREL
I'm not a neurotic actor.

HARDY
OK, OK, everybody loves you. Everybody thinks you're
a nice little boy. There.

LAUREL
I'm going.

*LAUREL exits. He comes back with a wax figure
of ABRAHAM LINCOLN.*

HARDY
Be careful!

LAUREL
It's not that fragile.

HARDY
There's the beginning of a crack around the nose.

LAUREL
So what, a crack around the nose?

HARDY
That's how it always starts.

LAUREL
What?

HARDY
After the nose, the eyes; after the eyes, the mouth; and
after the mouth, who knows?

   LAUREL touches the figure's face.

Don't touch it.

LAUREL
It's not going to melt.

   HARDY moves a small table.

More to the right.

HARDY
Like this?

LAUREL
A little more.

HARDY
Like this?

LAUREL
A hair to the left.

HARDY
Ah, you're annoying!

LAUREL
Why do you ask for my opinion?

HARDY positions the WAX FIGURE in front of the small table on which rests a notebook.

LAUREL & HARDY
He pointed at us as if he were selecting us out of a long line of losers.

The FIGURE raises its arm.

He said:

ABRAHAM LINCOLN
You. I know exactly what you're thinking. You're thinking: "Who does he think he is? He's been wasting our time for days. What does he want? We're professional actors. We know our job. We deserve consideration. We want lines. Great lines. We want characters. Great characters. What does he want and what's with this mysterious look on his face?" Am I right? Isn't that what you're thinking? Don't move! Stand still! I don't even want to see you blink. Nothing is more beautiful than stillness. When it stops. You understand? When it—something, anything—stops. But can actors like you do that? Huh? Simply stop. Simply

stop. Stick this into your head: Stillness brings a man closer to the beauty of the animal. Eyes shine, the skin tightens, nostrils dilate, blood finally becomes suspect. Do you understand? Don't move! All the people you see on the street hide, under their clothes, quiet and sluggish blood. Rosy blood. But in reality, it's a masquerade, a lie. Blood is always about to be shed.

HARDY
He opened his notebook. He read:

ABRAHAM LINCOLN
John Wilkes Booth—an actor who was enjoying playing Brutus in *Julius Caesar*—assassinated Abraham Lincoln with one shot. Abraham Lincoln with one shot. It was on April 14, 1865. 1865. The President of the United States was watching a play at Ford's Theatre in Washington D.C. The title of the play. The title of the play. Hardy, give me the title of the play that the sixteenth President of the United States was watching when he was assassinated by John Wilkes Booth. The title of the play, Hardy?

HARDY
I don't know. I didn't learn anything in school. Or if I did, I forgot it all.

LAUREL
I so wanted to know the title of the play. It would have impressed him. But who knows these things? Even a quiz-show freak wouldn't have been able to answer.

ABRAHAM LINCOLN
Our American Cousin. Our American Cousin. The play was called *Our American Cousin*, written by Tom Taylor. Who would remember this British writer if Abraham Lincoln hadn't been assassinated while

watching his play *Our American Cousin*? I wish the same luck on every playwright.

He closes his notebook.

HARDY
He closed his notebook.

LAUREL
Very loudly. Slam!

[3]

ABRAHAM LINCOLN
Let me introduce myself. I'm Scott Johnson. I've been hired by Leonard and Chris to play Abraham Lincoln's wax figure. I won't lie to you—I was very surprised by their offer. Everybody recognizes Leonard Brannigan and Chris Levine's talent. That's not the problem. Understand? But to play a wax figure is ... it's rather unusual. How should I personify it? Leonard and Chris reassured me. Under the wax, there was, of course, the sixteenth President of the United States. That's already something. Then, they enlightened me. Under the sixteenth President of the United States, there was another man. Mark Killman.

[4]

LAUREL
He wanted to scare us with this business about blood becoming suspect. We didn't move for how long?

HARDY
An hour.

LAUREL
More! A lot more. He was sitting at the small table, watching us. Not moving either. Nobody was moving. It was extraordinary. I have no other word for it. Three men. Not one moving. For more than an hour, a lot more than an hour. It was extraordinary.

HARDY
It was ... it wasn't ordinary.

LAUREL
Like I said. Who moved first?

HARDY
He did.

LAUREL
Yes. He said—

HARDY
He said: "You're a lot more interesting like this."

LAUREL
He said: "You're becoming like objects. If you keep this up, we'll want to fold you up and put you in a nice box. You're sweating like chairs under the sun. You're dripping like pianos under applause. You're slobbering like sponges. You're shining like cars."

HARDY
He said: "We're going to do nice things with you."

LAUREL
Then he exploded:

ABRAHAM LINCOLN
What are you doing? You don't get it! Who asked you to be meat? This bovine heaviness in your eyes—it's unhealthy. Making blood suspect, you can't do that, no, it's too much for TV actors. It makes me want to shove lines down your throat. Words! That's what you want! Words! Is there someone here who could die?

LAUREL
I was tempted to raise my hand. I often had the impulse to answer him with a gesture—raise my hand, as I mentioned, lower my head, close my eyes, wiggle my fingers.

ABRAHAM LINCOLN
Picture Abraham Lincoln's skull. His skull: The structure inside which everything happened! A .44 calibre bullet—shot from a cute little Deringer with a finely engraved grip—penetrates under the left ear and stops, intrigued, behind the right eye. What is this bullet doing? Huh? What is it up to, there, behind the presidential eye? This bullet is doing what you're not doing. It's doing what I want you to do. Hardy, look at Laurel. Can't you see the mask of ...

HARDY
Of ... I immediately thought—of ... death.

ABRAHAM LINCOLN
Of banality.

[5]

ABRAHAM LINCOLN
Like everybody, I discovered Leonard Brannigan and Chris Levine when they appeared in the TV series *Case*

Unclosed. A huge popular success. An immediate success like only television can produce. Leonard and Chris played a pair of detectives who made blunder after blunder, tripped on the carpet's flowers, caused their boss to lose his temper and in the end, always hit the jackpot. So, a series with a conventional and predictable plot that stole its juiciest ideas from other series. But Leonard and Chris were one heck of a duo. People loved them. Period. After the series, they were quickly forgotten. As if Leonard couldn't act without Chris and vice versa. When I heard those two were going to work with Mark Killman, I have to admit I was shocked. How could a director of Mark Killman's calibre work with two actors like Leonard Brannigan and Chris Levine? That was my question. There was, in that question, spite, disbelief, scorn, jealousy and maybe even some mental confusion. Mark Killman. For years, I had wanted to work with a director that exacting. The man intrigued me. No two of his shows were alike. The last one always shattered the previous one to pieces. Never had an artist elicited so much hate for his work and his person. Yes, Mark Killman was profoundly hated. But everybody wanted to work with him.

[6]

ABRAHAM LINCOLN
John Wilkes Booth, a fresh-faced teenager from Maryland, shows his palm to a gypsy. Hardy, you play the gypsy. Laurel, you play John.

HARDY
(*playing the gypsy*) Come! I'm seeing you for the first time but your presence is not new to me. Nor is your

adolescent smell, or your dark eyes—so young yet so old. Come closer! Come to me. Show me your hand since it's what you came for. My poor John! John Wilkes Booth. That's your name, isn't it? Your palm is bad—full of tears and blood. The lines disappear into a storm. The skin triggers unease, emotion. You still want to know? John, you'll break a lot of hearts. Those hearts—

ABRAHAM LINCOLN
Stay Greek. You're an oracle, a slab of flesh. Your mouth is the opening through which truth is going to make its way, like the bullet from the Deringer. You're full of information. A hen about to lay eggs!

HARDY
A hen?

ABRAHAM LINCOLN
Focus on one thing: Incubating the truth. To make it hatch. You, Laurel, you do this gesture where you brush your upper lip with the tips of your fingers. You're thirteen, you're throbbing. Do it!

LAUREL
I did it and while the tips of my fingers were creating John Wilkes Booth, an unknown emotion shifted a few bones inside me, making me almost come for no reason.

ABRAHAM LINCOLN
Let's take it again.

HARDY
Come! Let me look at your eyes. I've never seen such dark eyes blossom in such a pale face! John, you'll have fame. Your life will be short but intense. You'll end badly, very badly. Young man, I've never seen such a bad palm and I wish I hadn't seen it but if I were

younger, I would follow you to your crime because of
your beautiful face.

ABRAHAM LINCOLN
Too sentimental! When the hen is too heavy, it crushes
the eggs. Play it Greek! With granite! Transform!
Transform! Transform your mouth into a beak! I don't
give a damn about his angel skin or his dark eyes. He's
an actor first and a murderer second.

HARDY
Come! I'm seeing you for the first time but your
presence is not new to me. Nor is your adolescent smell,
or your dark eyes—so young yet so old. Come closer!
Come to me—

ABRAHAM LINCOLN
Too sentimental! Too much fuss! Dance!

HARDY
What?

ABRAHAM LINCOLN
On eggshells!

HARDY
I don't know how to dance!

ABRAHAM LINCOLN
Figure it out! Dance the death of Abraham Lincoln!
You saw it—a tiny red mark in the palm of his future
murderer. Come on, Hardy, politicize this thing! You're
not a woman anymore but a hen, a sphinx, a lottery,
understand? No? Do you know what black folks in
Georgia—tears rolling down their cheeks—screamed
when they heard about the assassination of the
President of the United States? "Massa Linkum is dead!
O Lord, Uncle Abe is dead! Massa Linkum is dead! O

Lord, Uncle Abe is dead!" Show some rhythm! Fire!
Dance!

[7]

ABRAHAM LINCOLN
There was a rumour that Leonard and Chris were
having an affair. You understand? Were involved. It was
only a rumour. As for Mark Killman, we knew very
little about his private life. He had published a book.
Obviously, I had read it. Slightly obscure but
fascinating. It hadn't done well at all but had left a
mark in the minds of a few people whose intelligence
couldn't be questioned. The book had the power to lead
fragile and depressed people to suicide. I'm
exaggerating. But ... in it, Mark Killman claimed,
somewhat pretentiously, that America was no longer a
country or even a continent but a way to do evil.
America wasn't concerned with the future and the
pursuit of freedom anymore. It was death wearing the
mask of stupidity. In the book, Mark Killman loathed
Hollywood, slaughtered its stars, vomited on its Golden
Calf. He also criticized war, which America was
manufacturing on an industrial scale. It's always easy to
criticize those who start wars. Who likes war? Critics
had faulted him for that ... easiness. In the end, nobody
knew what Mark Killman was trying to say with his
convoluted sentences. He was gently sent back to the
theatre and told that the publication of an essay
requires more depth and, most of all, more clarity.

LAUREL
Dance the death of Abraham Lincoln. What did he mean?

HARDY
What did he want me to do? I took a few steps.

LAUREL
Show what you did.

HARDY
That's not necessary.

LAUREL
Modesty? An actor like you?

HARDY
Don't push me.

LAUREL
You went like this.

LAUREL clumsily goes through the motions of an Eastern dance. HARDY hits him.

You're hurting me!

HARDY
You like it when I hurt you.

LAUREL
Then hit me again.

HARDY hits him, imitating the way HARDY used to torture LAUREL in their famous films.

ABRAHAM LINCOLN
Come here. Sit down.

HARDY
For the first time since the beginning of rehearsals, the three of us were sitting around the small table.

ABRAHAM LINCOLN
Listen. I get the feeling you don't know what you're doing. Am I right?

LAUREL
It's possible.

ABRAHAM LINCOLN
I asked you to dress like Laurel and Hardy. Do you know why?

LAUREL
To look like Laurel and Hardy.

ABRAHAM LINCOLN
To look like?

HARDY
Yes. We watch their films. We imitate them. We do our job. I've gained weight. Like a pig. For the role. I've gained ten pounds. My wife calls me crazy.

LAUREL
And I skip meals. To lose weight. My stomach hurts. I don't sleep well. When I sleep, I have nightmares. And yesterday, he really hurt me. He stuck his finger in my eye. I thought I was going to pass out.

HARDY
I didn't do it on purpose.

LAUREL
You're not focused.

ABRAHAM LINCOLN
You think to play fatness you just need to be fat?

LAUREL & HARDY
What?

ABRAHAM LINCOLN
You think to play thinness you just need to be thin? The
truth lies in the idea of fatness and in the idea of
thinness. Otherwise, it's garbage. Don't look at me like
that!

LAUREL
I admit it. I was looking at him with astonishment
mixed perhaps with some kind of ... of desire.

HARDY
What are you talking about? You're trying to make
yourself interesting? It's pathetic.

LAUREL
I'm not a dog. I have the right to open my heart.

HARDY
Disgusting.

LAUREL
What?

HARDY
What you say. Open your heart. Shut your trap instead.

LAUREL
Do you want to know what I feel for you?

ABRAHAM LINCOLN
Careful. I can hear you think. You persist in thinking
that fatness and thinness are only a matter of quantity.

More of this, less of that. Look at this fat notebook. Do you think I wrote miles of notes to end up with this?

LAUREL
He pointed at us.

HARDY
It's true.

LAUREL
He stayed like that, pointing at us, for quite a while. Without batting an eye.

HARDY
That's also true.

LAUREL
How long?

HARDY
Two minutes.

LAUREL
Maybe more. Two minutes being pointed at in silence. It's …

HARDY
It's a rare event.

LAUREL
How can one describe one's feelings in a moment like that?

ABRAHAM LINCOLN
American fatness is not just a matter of fat. There's more than fried chicken and cow dung patties in American fatness. I want to be clear. Very clear. Let me read to you what I wrote about American fatness.

LAUREL & HARDY
Instead of opening his notebook, he got up. He made strange moves. He said:

ABRAHAM LINCOLN
Imagine a bottomless heart. Stuffed with a seventy-storey skyscraper, a megalopolis and its suicidal suburbs, and added on top of this junk, the countless thoughts that weigh down the man in the street at each of his steps. A heart that pumps like a hungry machine. A heart that eats, shits and doesn't know why. That swallows the skies and spits back emptiness. American fatness is a cancer.

LAUREL
He made more moves.

HARDY
Moves like ... Strange moves.

LAUREL
Not that strange. It's just that ... that they were moves from ... from somewhere else. Asian moves. No doubt.

ABRAHAM LINCOLN
American thinness is a trap. A fishhook cast in the eyes of newborns.

LAUREL & HARDY
Newborns?

ABRAHAM LINCOLN
Yes. American newborns are caught by the eye, pulled from their digestive torpor and thrown, still flapping about, onto the sets of commercials. Commercials for diapers. Diapers that will absorb their innocence down to the last drop. America loses weight only to rake in money. It's a thinness that hides a fatness. So?

LAUREL & HARDY
   So?

ABRAHAM LINCOLN
   Can you play that?

[10   ]

ABRAHAM LINCOLN
   At the beginning of rehearsals with Leonard and Chris,
   I googled Mark Killman. I discovered some things.
   Mark Killman had spent some time in Asia. One site
   said he had studied Noh theatre in Japan. Another site
   contradicted that information. Or completed it in a
   way. It said that Mark Killman had disappeared for
   several months in India. The source of that information
   was a book written by a journalist who had met him in
   the caves of Rishikesh while she was practising yoga.
   What was Mark Killman doing at the foot of the
   Himalayas? She didn't specify. She only mentioned that
   she had met him. At the time, of course, Mark Killman
   was nothing more than a young man with long hair.

[11   ]

HARDY
   After three weeks of rehearsals, my wife started to
   suspect me of something. Hard to put a finger on what.
   I was showing up late. I couldn't make myself go
   straight home from work. I would go drinking.

LAUREL
   With me. Say it. It's not a crime.

HARDY
It's true.

LAUREL
And we would talk.

HARDY
About Mark, his way of working, this thing that
fascinated him: Lincoln in a theatre assassinated by an
actor.

LAUREL
My eyes would fill with tears that constantly threatened
to fall into my beer. It had nothing to do with the
assassination of anybody, much less of a U.S. President.
I felt on the brink of discovering terrible things. About
myself. And, you know ... you know that after being
slapped by you, having my ass kicked by you, even if it
were to better immerse ourselves in the deeply sadistic
dynamic of Laurel and Hardy—that's what he
explained while raising his arm. Remember? Like this,
his arm. Up with his fist clenched. Probably a tic. But
there are tics and there are tics. This particular tic
impressed me. A gesture that meant nothing but invited
reflection. So he explained, with his arm like this, that
the truth of any human relationship can be reduced to
two things: Sadism and masochism. Between these two
extremes, everything can be found in the realm of
human affairs: Love, friendship, contempt, hate,
adoration ... so ... so ... you must know I ended up
feeling an array of emotions for you ...

HARDY
You talk like him.

LAUREL
What?

HARDY
An array of emotions.

LAUREL
Hit me.

HARDY
I'm tired.

[12]

ABRAHAM LINCOLN
How do you play a wax figure? How do you play
Abraham Lincoln? How do you play the wax of a
figure that represents Abraham Lincoln? How do you
play Abraham Lincoln cast in wax? Most of all, how do
you play Mark Killman hidden under layers of skin and
wax? These are the questions I was throwing at Chris
and Leonard. I had never played with a fake beard. It
was an additional reason for accepting their offer.
Actors sometimes agree to do the impossible for stupid
reasons. It's their right. And they had reassured me
about at least one thing: The goal wasn't to look like
Mark Killman or Abraham Lincoln's figure. They were
not talking about resemblance. But about imitation.
They even insisted that the imitation had to be
laborious, clumsy, grotesque. An imitation that would
expose the baseness of all imitations. Mark Killman had
told them repeatedly that we're living in a time when
the imitator is more important than the imitated. The
truth, when subjected to extreme transformations, can't
hold up to the flashiest lie.

HARDY
My mother told me on her deathbed that her only
pleasure in life had been to eat. With this one short
sentence, she crossed out love. I, her son, was worth
less than a good meal. Sad conclusion to a life. That
day, I lost a lot of illusions. And I became an actor.
Why? So I could eat my characters. I discovered that
recently. And when Mark Killman chose me to play the
part of Hardy, I understood that he had grasped an
essential part of my personality. An obvious part, it's
true, but as they say, not everyone has eyes to see.

LAUREL
My turn. I want to confide too.

HARDY
You don't have to do everything I do. Give me some
space.

LAUREL
No. I don't want to give you space.

HARDY
Leave me alone. I still have things to say.

LAUREL
Say them.

HARDY
They concern you and I don't want you to hear.

LAUREL
I'm an adult.

HARDY
That's the problem.

LAUREL
What do you mean?

HARDY
You know very well.

LAUREL
Hold me in your arms, I'm cold.

He does.

[14]

ABRAHAM LINCOLN
Laurel.

LAUREL
Yes?

ABRAHAM LINCOLN
I want you to be handsome. Magnetic. You understand?
I want the assassin to be irresistible.

LAUREL
Absolutely. Like this.

ABRAHAM LINCOLN
Not quite. John Wilkes Booth was a ladies' man. He
attracted them. The young, the not so young and the
old. He also attracted certain men. But at the time, you
understand ... Anyway, a painful magnetism emanated
from his eyes, which were deep and dark. He had slept
with a lot of actresses, including Laura Keene. On April
14, 1865, Laura Keene was playing the role of Florence
Trenchard in *Our American Cousin.*

HARDY
By Tom Taylor.

ABRAHAM LINCOLN
Shut up. A role she had created in New York a few
years earlier. Laura Keene would have given anything
for a night with John Wilkes Booth. Hardy.

HARDY
Yes?

ABRAHAM LINCOLN
You're going to play hope. We're in New York. Let's
say a few months before the assassination of the
President. Laura Keene has just left the stage. She enters
her dressing room, still dizzy from applause. Someone
opens the door. It's John. She hasn't seen him in
months. She hopes. Play that. Only that.

LAUREL & HARDY
Only what?

ABRAHAM LINCOLN
The hope of a night. The painful magnetism of dark
eyes.

LAUREL looks at HARDY with love.

[15]

LAUREL
One day, he showed up with a fake beard and a wig.
The next day, he was wearing a frock coat. The day
after that, he had a waxen complexion.

HARDY
High-quality make-up.

LAUREL
Within a few days, Mark had taken on the appearance
of Abraham Lincoln.

HARDY
Of his wax figure.

LAUREL
You're right.

HARDY
Mark always insisted he wanted to look like a figure,
not like a man.

LAUREL
Subtle difference, he kept repeating. Subtle difference.

HARDY
We finally understood he wanted to be in the show
with us.

LAUREL
He had given himself the role of the dead man.

HARDY
Of the victim. Of the assassinated.

ABRAHAM LINCOLN
Isn't it immoral for assassins to be sexually attractive
and have magnetic eyes? Shouldn't assassins look like
assassins and provoke only disgust? What do you
think?

LAUREL
I need to think about it.

HARDY
Me too.

ABRAHAM LINCOLN
You have no balls.

[16]

ABRAHAM LINCOLN
At first, I had a strong reaction. To the make-up. The
skin on my face broke out in red patches. I had dizzy
spells, was short of breath. And my neck was itchy. I
asked myself: "What did you get yourself into, Scott?" I
don't like to suffer. Is it banal to admit that? No. A lot
of people like to suffer. Actors for instance. I was
baptized. I threw away God. What do I have left? Art?
The red patches on my face changed my approach to
theatre. I told myself: "You have an allergy. Like
millions of people. Poor man. Poor little thing. And you
pretend to not be who you are when you perform. So?"
So? Nothing. I went to work. Very quickly, I realized
the character of Abraham Lincoln didn't interest me. It
was John Wilkes Booth I was fascinated with. I was
trying to understand him. I was projecting myself. I was
seeing myself at twenty-six again. Who was the
President of the United States then? It didn't matter. I
imagined approaching him in his box while he was
watching *Death of a Salesman*. Would I have pulled the
trigger? And most importantly, why would I have done
it? Why?

[17]

LAUREL
He started coughing. Violent fits. Rehearsals were
becoming embarrassing.

HARDY
You were afraid of catching his germs.

LAUREL
I know myself. I get the flu, it turns into bronchitis. It takes me months to get over it. For an actor, it's hell.

HARDY
For anybody.

LAUREL
I know what I mean.

HARDY
Once, he fainted. I had to pick him up by myself.

LAUREL
You're still mad at me? I didn't want to touch him.

HARDY
Germs. That's what I said.

LAUREL
No. Something else. I don't know what. Something.

HARDY
When I picked him up to put him back in his chair, I got a shock. A small electric shock. It startled me. I dropped him on the floor.

LAUREL
Now it was you who didn't want to touch him.

LAUREL & HARDY
We moved closer. We leaned over. We saw. We saw water coming out of his face. Water shining on the wax. A lot of water. Mark Killman was sweating bullets under his make-up.

ABRAHAM LINCOLN
I also googled Scott Johnson. I wanted to know if I
existed. I found twenty-seven Scott Johnsons. Then I
googled John Wilkes Booth. I found excerpts from his
diary which he wrote as the most wanted man in the
United States. After his crime, he managed to escape on
horseback. His leg was hurting. His leg. Why did John
Wilkes Booth write that his leg was hurting? I googled ...
I googled ... I don't remember ... maybe I googled "leg
of John Wilkes Booth?" I discovered that John—who I
was starting to fall for despite his crime—injured
himself at Ford's Theatre. After shooting the President,
he leapt from the balcony onto the stage. In his fall, he
fractured a leg. Then he took the pose of a tragic actor
and, addressing the audience, shouted: "*Sic semper
tyrannis!*" Thus ever to tyrants! For a moment, the
audience thought this theatrical audacity was part of
Our American Cousin. But Laura Keene—who was
playing the role of Florence Trenchard—knew it wasn't.
When she recognized John who was fleeing backstage,
she opened her mouth and screamed, screamed,
screamed.

ABRAHAM LINCOLN
Applause!

We hear applause.

Laura Keene leaves the stage under a shower of
applause. She's drenched. She's sweating under her
enormous skirt. A skirt with a twenty-foot diameter.

(*to HARDY*) Show me how a nineteenth-century woman moves through space with such an outfit.

LAUREL
I can do it. Mark, let me try.

ABRAHAM LINCOLN
Shut up. Back to your place. Don't move.

LAUREL
Can I breathe, at least?

ABRAHAM LINCOLN
Hardy, go ahead.

HARDY complies.

LAUREL
Pathetic.

ABRAHAM LINCOLN
Would you shut up! What's the matter with you today?

HARDY
Yes, you're annoying. And on top of that, you stink.

LAUREL
I'm not the one who farts like a pack mule.

HARDY
No, but you belch, and it's hell.

LAUREL
My stomach hurts. You have no compassion. How many times have I told you I have ulcers?

HARDY
In your head.

LAUREL

Yes, ulcers in my head! And you, you have sphincters in your head. Whether you think or shit, you get the same thing!

HARDY

You're going to die alone like a rat. You know why? Because you're insufferable.

LAUREL

And you? Do you know what I hear about you? You're done as an actor. If I hadn't been here these past few years, you would be advertizing laxatives. Mr. Asshole! That's what people would call you! Mom, Mom, come see! It's Mr. Asshole on the sidewalk. Look, he's crossing the street. Can I ask him for an autograph? Yes, but be careful. I heard he can't hold it in anymore!

*They start to hit each other. The applause fades.
Stops. The silence drains any motivation from
their fight. They look at each other, dazed.*

ABRAHAM LINCOLN

Play the scene. Laura Keene enters her dressing room. Someone knocks right away. She opens. It's John Wilkes Booth.

HARDY

(*playing Laura Keene*) John! What are you doing in New York?

LAUREL

(*playing John Wilkes Booth*) I came to see you perform.

HARDY

You were in the audience tonight! You should have warned me. I would have performed for you. Only for you.

LAUREL
　　You were sublime, Laura.

HARDY
　　You really think so? Oh, John! I'm so happy to see you!
　　I can't believe it. You, here, tonight, in my small
　　dressing room! But let me look at you. You're pale.

LAUREL
　　Give me your hand. I've dreamt about this moment for
　　so long.

HARDY
　　Where have you been? It's been months since I last
　　heard from you.

LAUREL
　　Laura, listen to me. Very soon, I'm going to play the
　　most important role of my career.

HARDY
　　Hamlet! You're finally going to play Hamlet!

LAUREL
　　Even better. Hamlet hesitates, stammers. But I'll get
　　straight to the point. I'll say everything in a single
　　action.

HARDY
　　You're shaking.

LAUREL
　　Fame, Laura. It's the shiver of fame. And the spectre of
　　the abyss awaiting me.

HARDY
　　John, why do you shroud yourself in so much mystery?

LAUREL
  I can't tell you any more. In Washington, you'll know
  everything.

HARDY
  In Washington?

LAUREL
  Aren't you playing in *Our American Cousin* in
  Washington? At Ford's Theatre, I believe?

HARDY
  That's right. And you know what? It will be the
  thousandth time that I'll play Florence Trenchard. And
  you know what? It will be on April 14. And you know
  what? April 14 is Good Friday.

LAUREL
  I'll be there.

HARDY
  Good Friday. It's exciting, isn't it?

LAUREL
  It will probably be the least exciting thing of that day.

HARDY
  Why do you say that?

LAUREL
  I want to make love to you.

HARDY
  Here? Now? But ...

  *LAUREL moves toward HARDY to kiss him. He
  is encumbered by HARDY's enormous imaginary
  skirt.*

Just a moment, I'll take it off.

LAUREL
Take everything off.

HARDY
Oh, John!

[20]

ABRAHAM LINCOLN
I stupidly fell in love with an assassin. I continued my research on Google. John Wilkes Booth, after his exploit at Ford's Theatre, managed to escape on horseback. The greatest manhunt in the entire history of the United States had begun. Never has a man been as hunted as he. I spent many delectable hours imagining John, on the run, hiding in foul-smelling swamps, savagely bitten by squadrons of mosquitoes diving on his broken leg. He must have suffered atrociously. At night, he was shivering, his boots filled with mud, his feet wet. During the day, his rags were drenched in sweat. A sweat full of fear. Full of paranoia. I would contemplate his deep eyes for long hours thanks to photos found on the internet. Dark, watery eyes shining with sadness. I would admire his moustache. His tragic actor's pose with his chest a little thrown out. But most of all … I could spend hours imagining his death.

ABRAHAM LINCOLN
John Wilkes Booth. He's the show's enigma. Why
would a twenty-six-year-old actor, who was considered
the most handsome man of his time, assassinate the
President of the United States? What does the bullet
from his Deringer destroy exactly, once lodged in
Abraham Lincoln's skull? What does it unhinge? What
does it scream all the way from 1865? It still whistles. It
has gone through many skulls. Yet it still whistles. OK.
Get up and play a scene.

LAUREL & HARDY
Which one?

ABRAHAM LINCOLN
The one Abraham Lincoln is watching when his
assassin's bullet whispers in his ear that reality may
only be the flip side of fiction. Don't forget one thing:
It's Good Friday. April 14, 1865 is Good Friday. You
can check it in an almanac.

LAUREL
Yes, we know, Mark. You've said it already.

ABRAHAM LINCOLN
Shut up. Let's go over it again. Just as Abraham Lincoln
enters his box at Ford's Theatre in Washington, the
musicians start "Hail to the Chief." The military
fanfare reserved for the President. Junk brass. You want
to hear? Listen.

We hear an excerpt of the military fanfare.

The entire audience rises. The President sits with his
wife Mary. Tom Taylor's famous play begins.

LAUREL & HARDY
Our American Cousin.

ABRAHAM LINCOLN
(*with a sudden and growing rage*) I know. We know.
Our American Cousin. No need to hit us over the head
with it. Everybody knows. What play was Abraham
Lincoln watching when he fell into a coma, a bullet in
his skull? The answer? *Our American Cousin.* Yes. *Our
American Cousin.* A platitude that Laura Keene played
more than a thousand times. She was thirty when she
created the role of Florence Trenchard. The role of an
ingénue, which she performed until she was forty. But
that didn't stop John Wilkes Booth from showering her
with compliments, from ripping off her skirt, which
could have concealed a grand piano—pianist
included—and from doing to her what he was doing
left and right and more often centre. *Our American
Cousin.* Yes. A comedy which became a national
tragedy. Or is it the opposite? By the way. On the
subject of comedy, I have a thought to share with you.
About fatness and thinness. Again. What can I say, I'm
obsessed. Take a fat guy. Take a thin guy. Rub them
together. What do you get?

LAUREL
No. I had no desire to answer that. Plus, I knew I
would never get it right. Better to keep my mouth shut.

ABRAHAM LINCOLN
You get comedy. And if you scratch the comedy, what
do you discover? The hideous mask of …

LAUREL & HARDY
Of banality.

ABRAHAM LINCOLN
No. Of death.

The military fanfare stops.

[22]

HARDY
I couldn't understand why Mark insisted that I play
women's roles. The gypsy who reads the palm of
Lincoln's future murderer. A *cliché*. And this Laura
Keene. I know. In a film, when an actor plays a woman,
it's a guaranteed Oscar nomination. But with my
physique ...

LAUREL
Mark wanted to emphasize the ridiculousness of the
situation. Easy. With you as a woman, it was in the bag.

HARDY
And with you as a woman?

LAUREL
With me? I would have done better than an actress.

HARDY
Yes. And I know why.

LAUREL
Why?

HARDY
It's better if I don't answer.

LAUREL
What are you afraid of?

HARDY
    Forget it.

LAUREL
    By the way, how are your two daughters? Sandra and
    Lea this, Sandra and Lea that. You used to talk about
    them all the time.

HARDY
    Used to?

LAUREL
    Used to. When we were shooting *Case Unclosed*.

HARDY
    They're doing well. They're growing.

LAUREL
    What's the matter, Leonard?

HARDY
    Nothing. I don't like the way you look at me.

LAUREL
    When? Now?

HARDY
    Forget it.

LAUREL
    What are you afraid of?

ABRAHAM LINCOLN
    Let's do it again.

LAUREL & HARDY
    What?

ABRAHAM LINCOLN
    Everything.

HARDY

Toward the end, he wasn't reading from his notebook anymore.

LAUREL

That's right. We wouldn't hear the Slam! I had a feeling he was losing it.

HARDY

He had a fever, that's for sure.

LAUREL

He was coughing, spitting. Sometimes, he would fall asleep in the middle of rehearsal. It was embarrassing. The great Mark Killman was snoring in front of his actors.

HARDY

Disturbing. Because ... because when he was asleep, he looked strikingly like Abraham Lincoln's figure.

LAUREL

And often, he would wake up with a start—

HARDY

—and go on talking as if nothing had happened.

LAUREL

He was improvising. He would tell stories about the Civil War.

HARDY

Slavery. The schizophrenia of America.

LAUREL

The stupidity of America.

LAUREL & HARDY
He would say:

ABRAHAM LINCOLN
Everything started with an actor. And everything will
end with an actor. Why did John Wilkes Booth
assassinate the sixteenth President of the United States?
Why does one assassinate a U.S. President? For political
reasons? Who, today, would want to assassinate a U.S.
President?

HARDY
An actor?

ABRAHAM LINCOLN
Tom Cruise?

LAUREL
Al Pacino.

ABRAHAM LINCOLN
Shut up. Why would he do it? What has changed in the
world since April 14, 1865? War, of course, never
changes. What would the world be if there were no
wars? No, that will never change. Laurel and Hardy.

LAUREL & HARDY
Yes?

ABRAHAM LINCOLN
I feel you're not grasping the essential. Not
understanding the question. And the question is? Is?
Don't both answer at the same time! You have no balls.
Let me repeat it. The question is: Why did John Wilkes
Booth assassinate Abraham Lincoln? Because Booth
was against the abolition of slavery? Because he
supported the values of the South? But how can anyone
be in favour of slavery? How can anyone agree, in good

conscience, to chain men from dawn to dusk, raise them like cattle, mate them like cattle, force them to work in cotton fields, with their nails torn out, make them sleep in dog houses? How can we call those values? American values!

[24]

LAUREL

The doctor had warned me. I needed to take a vacation. Or to get off coffee. I got off coffee. Anyway, I was under contract with Killman. And I've always respected my contracts. I'm a professional actor. As a professional actor, I feel obligated to rehearse and perform even sick as a dog. I was hoping—it's true—that Killman would cancel rehearsals. Because to be fair, he looked even sicker than me. At first, I thought it was a tactic on his part. He was playing sick to manipulate us. He wanted us to feel sorry for him. But. But I adored his sadistic way of directing me. And frankly, I could have done without his delirious rantings and his snoring. I was starting to seriously doubt the whole business. What were we going to show the public? I wanted to talk about it with Leonard after rehearsals. But he had changed too. He was avoiding me. It was starting to feel like a train wreck. I couldn't understand anything anymore. And in bed at night, I would cry.

[25]

ABRAHAM LINCOLN

Leonard and Chris had told me—in a rather clumsy way I must say—the story of Tom Taylor's play *Our*

American Cousin. They themselves had never read it.
They only knew it through the words of Mark Killman.
In fact, Killman had told them the play didn't have a
real importance for the show he had in mind. Lincoln
was watching it when the radar screen of his mind had
shut down. Yes. But he could have been watching
Shakespeare's *Julius Caesar* and it wouldn't have
changed the trajectory of the bullet. I amused myself
trying to find the last words Lincoln heard before he
was shot. It was a line of Asa Trenchard's, the actual
American cousin from the title. Here it is: "Don't know
the manners of good society, eh? Well, I guess I know
enough to turn you inside out, old gal—you
sockdologizing old man-trap!" He was saying this line
to an old lady who was criticizing him for acting like a
Yankee bull in an English china shop. "Don't know the
manners of good society, eh? Well, I guess I know
enough to turn you inside out, old gal—you
sockdologizing old man-trap!" And it's on that note
that Abraham Lincoln bowed out.

[26]

HARDY
My two daughters had the flu. My wife was making
scenes. Mark Killman's health was deteriorating in
front of our eyes. I didn't know what to think anymore.
Chris was behaving strangely. I couldn't tell him
anything. He would lose his temper. I wanted to slap
him. But I controlled myself. I kept watching Laurel
and Hardy films and couldn't see why Chris and I had
to draw inspiration from them for our performance. He
had forced us to rehearse dressed like them. We spent
hours perfecting our slaps and our kicks in the ass. I
have an open mind—I've been around—but there are

limits, even in the theatre. I asked Mark several times. He always answered that in the twenty-first century, we can't afford to show historical facts on stage as if they are actual historical facts. History is just one more hoax and theatre doesn't have to reproduce it. Then why Laurel and Hardy?

ABRAHAM LINCOLN
Because they're perfect. I don't want you to play John Wilkes Booth getting ready to assassinate Abraham Lincoln, you understand? I want you to play Stan Laurel playing John Wilkes Booth getting ready to assassinate Abraham Lincoln's wax figure.

LAUREL
Yes, Mark. I understand.

ABRAHAM LINCOLN
And you, at that moment, I want you to play Oliver Hardy playing Harry Hawk ...

HARDY
Harry Hawk?

ABRAHAM LINCOLN
The actor who was playing Asa Trenchard on April 14, 1865. Is that clear? I want you to play Oliver Hardy playing Harry Hawk playing Asa Trenchard. You know the line?

HARDY
"Don't know the manners of good society, eh? Well, I guess I know enough to turn you inside out, old gal— you sockdologizing old man-trap!"

ABRAHAM LINCOLN
Then what are you whining about? You know the line. Just play it.

[27]

ABRAHAM LINCOLN
   Like everyone, I heard about Mark Killman's death on
TV. I have to admit it was a shock. I didn't know him
personally. I had, of course, heard a lot about him.
More bad than good, it goes without saying. But I knew
a large part of the mean and perverse things attributed
to him were exaggerated and likely made up by those
who envied him or didn't have his talent, let alone his
genius. Chris Levine and Leonard Brannigan were all
over the media. They had the honour of having worked
with him on his final show. What had Mark Killman's
last moments been? What was he working on? What
did he die of? These were the kinds of questions
Leonard and Chris were being asked. They seemed
really upset. We finally learned that Mark Killman had
died from an aggressive cancer. Nobody understood
how, up to the last moment, he had been able to stand
on his two legs, tolerate the make-up sessions he put
himself through to look like his character, direct
actors—in short, make theatre—instead of dying in his
bed. It brought tears to my eyes. So you understand my
profound emotion when, only a few weeks after his
death, I got a call from Chris Levine. He was offering
me the opportunity to be in the show Mark Killman
was directing before he died.

[28]

HARDY
   He said: "I'll be back in half an hour. I'm going to get
coffee."

LAUREL
But he stayed exactly where he was. In the chair, behind
the small table.

HARDY
What were we to do?

LAUREL
Yes, what were we to do? We were used to that kind of
behaviour. But that day—I don't know why—there was
something in the air ...

HARDY
Something like gravity.

LAUREL
If you want. Gravity.

HARDY
I want, yes.

LAUREL
Whatever you want.

HARDY
That's right. Whatever I want.

LAUREL
He was staring.

HARDY
He was breathing in short gasps.

LAUREL
How long did we stay like that, transfixed, in silence?

HARDY
An eternity. But it wasn't in silence.

LAUREL

It was a kind of silence. You know how it was, he had
made a habit of that kind of silence. And it was in that
kind of silence that he would make strange gestures.
Raise an arm. Or something. A gesture that meant
nothing. Something to intrigue us. But I wasn't biting
anymore.

HARDY

You're getting on my nerves. He said: "Yankees.
Confederates. The Civil War. Slavery. You have no
balls. You never think about these things. You're
monkeys. You drool. You belch. You make me dizzy
because you're incapable of concentrating. What I want
is a clarity of movement. A clarity of tone. A clarity of
gaze. Precision. Economy. You're killing me."

LAUREL

You're a pain in the ass. He said: "Yankees.
Confederates. A war between brothers. Thousands of
dead bodies that cover the earth with their wounds. An
America—puritanical, rotten, schizophrenic, vicious,
thirsty for evil as much as for good … an America
concentrated in the brain of its President. What a
prodigious fruit to burst, right? The most beautiful of
temptations. Let me tell you: Killing is nothing. But
enslaving a man, that's the heart of the matter. It's
killing a man while keeping him alive."

ABRAHAM LINCOLN

You understand? It's killing a man while keeping him
alive. No, you don't understand? You have to make up
your mind. Are you a man of the North or a man of the
South? You need to know. Because that changes
everything. What do you want? Huh? Being an artist
doesn't give you the right to not know what you want.
Who do you want to kill? Who do you choose to riddle

with bullets? To blow up with his entire family? Who, in your eyes, has the honour of being the object of your ineradicable hate? No answer. I'm going to tell you one more thing. Your answer, if it exists somewhere, is of no importance. There. Now tell me if I'm right. No answer. I'm not right. I'm rarely right about most important things. That's why I'm in the theatre. Because there are too many people on this earth who are right. Who want to be right at any cost. Who would rather die than not be right. Who prefer to blow up everything because they can't stand being told they're not right. Am I right? No answer. I'm going to tell you one more thing. John Wilkes Booth killed Abraham Lincoln because he was an actor. That's all.

HARDY
And it's on that note that he died.

ABRAHAM LINCOLN
He really said that before he died?

LAUREL
More or less.

HARDY
Not exactly.

LAUREL
But more or less.

HARDY
Actually, he didn't die right after saying that.

LAUREL
That's true. He got up.

HARDY
Painfully. I wanted to help him.

LAUREL
You didn't.

HARDY
No. I only wanted to. Because—

LAUREL
Because we couldn't help him anymore. That must be why.

HARDY
Maybe. We were afraid to move closer.

ABRAHAM LINCOLN
Why? The man was about to die.

LAUREL & HARDY
We didn't know!

ABRAHAM LINCOLN
But it was clear he was very sick.

LAUREL & HARDY
Not that clear.

ABRAHAM LINCOLN
So what happened? He got up and ...?

LAUREL
You won't believe it, Scott.

ABRAHAM LINCOLN
What?

LAUREL
Tell him.

HARDY
Mark started to ... to dance.

ABRAHAM LINCOLN
To dance?

HARDY
A sort of dance.

LAUREL
Something vaguely Asian. But really sad.

HARDY
Yes. Really sad.

ABRAHAM LINCOLN
Why?

LAUREL
Because it was so painful to watch. It was as if he were
unravelling bit by bit. His eyes ... his eyes ... it was
horrible ...

HARDY
Horrible, yes. And embarrassing. An artist like Mark,
to die like that.

ABRAHAM LINCOLN
Like that, how?

HARDY
Dancing in a grotesque manner.

LAUREL
An absurd manner. Ugly manner. He was drooling, you
see.

HARDY
His face red, his body all shrivelled up.

LAUREL
It was pouring out of every pore. His make-up, his skin,
his sweat—it was all mixing together, it was dripping, it
was disgusting and incredibly sad.

ABRAHAM LINCOLN
He died dancing?

LAUREL & HARDY
Yes, dancing.

HARDY
Show him.

LAUREL
Like this. More or less like this.

[29]

ABRAHAM LINCOLN
I read Mark Killman's large notebook several times. He
had written on the first page, in big letters: *John Wilkes
Booth Goes to the Theatre*. I immediately thought that
was the title of the show Mark had intended to do. I
asked Leonard and Chris. They told me Mark hadn't
discussed a title with them. They had rehearsed for
weeks without really knowing what they were
rehearsing. Did Mark have a clear idea of what he
wanted? Very quickly, in working with Leonard and
Chris, I realized we couldn't answer that question. The
tribute show we wanted to create wouldn't be his, but
ours. It was up to Leonard, Chris and me to give
meaning to Mark's death. I suggested we call our show
Mark Killman Goes to the Theatre. It would present the
rehearsals of Mark Killman's unfinished show and the
grand finale would be his own death. Leonard and

Chris had thought the idea brilliant. Curiously, from that moment on, I became their director. And more and more, every day, Leonard and Chris were getting on my nerves.

[30]

HARDY

I never should have gotten involved in this. I never should have accepted Mark's offer. I knew from the beginning something wasn't right. Why would a director like Mark be interested in an actor like me? It's all Chris's fault. He's the one who twisted my arm. Why, why didn't I leave after Mark's death? A tribute show! What a pretentious idea! And Scott Johnson! What a pain! What made Chris think of him? He's using us to boost his career. He's using Mark's death to … Argh! There are days when we shouldn't get so much as a toe out of bed. I just wish—

LAUREL

You talk to yourself now?

HARDY

I'm rehearsing my role.

LAUREL

Which one?

HARDY

Give me some space, Chris. I feel like you're spying on me. I can't even go to the bathroom without having you follow me like a dog.

LAUREL

That's love.

HARDY
    I don't appreciate that kind of humour.

LAUREL
    That's humour.

[31]

ABRAHAM LINCOLN
    Rehearsals for the tribute show were turning into a
    disaster. I couldn't concentrate. I wanted to be perfect.
    To be up to the task. Anticipate everything. Know
    everything. I had forgotten that theatre—although
    performed under bright lights—expresses above all a
    sense of mystery and darkness. Who, in life, can totally
    comprehend who they are and what they do? Nobody.
    So how could mere characters accomplish this feat?

[32]

LAUREL
    In my opinion, we should focus on the assassination
    scene. Mark often talked about the trajectory of the
    bullet. It had lodged itself behind the President's right
    eye.

HARDY
    So? How does that affect the scene? It could have
    lodged itself behind the left eye or the nose or the
    forehead or whatever the hell! How is that going to
    change my way of saying, "Don't know the manners of
    good society, eh? Well, I guess I know enough to turn
    you inside out, old gal—you sockdologizing old man-
    trap!"

LAUREL
Calm down! I'm simply explaining to Scott how Mark
was imagining the scene. If he insisted on the trajectory
of the bullet, he must have had his reasons. You know
very well how each gesture was important to him. And
believe it or not, I'm the one who has to hold the
Deringer. So I need to know how to hold it, and exactly
where to put it in the back of Lincoln's head.

HARDY
Lincoln's figure.

LAUREL
What about Lincoln's figure?

HARDY
Mark insisted that in his show, Booth doesn't
assassinate Lincoln, but Lincoln's figure. Subtle
difference.

LAUREL
Since when are you interested in subtle differences?

HARDY
What do you think I am? A moron? I'll have you know
that Mark never would have hired you if it weren't for
me. And you never, never would have been in *Case
Unclosed* if I hadn't insisted that they take you. Never!

LAUREL
I can't believe I'm hearing these lies! Your deep
insecurity and total mediocrity make you ... make
you ...

HARDY
Make me what?

LAUREL
Leonard, do we have to stoop this low in front of Scott?

HARDY
Oh, I had completely forgotten about him!

ABRAHAM LINCOLN
I'm going to get coffee. I'll be back. I'll be back in half an hour.

LAUREL & HARDY
That's right. Come back in half an hour.

[33]

ABRAHAM LINCOLN
I didn't sleep much during that period. And when I did sleep, I had strange dreams. I would wake up feeling like I had escaped great danger. Basically, I dreamt I was being pursued. It couldn't have been clearer: I was reliving John Wilkes Booth's fear when the whole of America was after him. I managed to convince myself that John Wilkes Booth's last moments would help me understand, or grasp, Abraham Lincoln's last moments and perhaps even Mark Killman's last moments.

[34]

HARDY
I couldn't believe it. I invited my wife to her favourite restaurant, a seafood restaurant. I wanted to tell her the news over dessert. I couldn't believe it. I had been offered a leading role in an American film, to be shot here. But the best part was that I was going to co-star with Al Pacino. I just couldn't believe it.

ABRAHAM LINCOLN
John Wilkes Booth's last moments. Here's how it happened: After many incidents, Booth takes refuge in a barn where tobacco is drying. About thirty soldiers surround him. It's night. Lieutenant Colonel Conger threatens to burn the barn if Booth doesn't give himself up. Ten minutes later, the barn is set on fire. It lights up from the inside, revealing the fugitive's shadow through the planks. Conger mentions in his report that Booth appeared to him like an Apollo in flames. Is it in the natural order of things for a Lieutenant Colonel of the First District of Columbia Cavalry to see an Apollo in flames in a starving, wounded and asphyxiating man, living the last moments of his life?

[36]

HARDY
I just couldn't believe it. My wife either. She asked if she could share the news with her family, her friends. If the newspapers were going to talk about it. I told her it was top secret, that we had to wait until everything was signed. She promised to keep the secret. We had another dessert. And right then, anxiety grabbed me in its claws.

[37]

ABRAHAM LINCOLN
Conger also mentions that Booth drops his rifle in order to grab a pistol and put it to his head. Then, gunshot.

The bullet goes in under the right ear and comes out the neck. It severs three cervical vertebrae, paralyzing Booth. Did he want to die like a hero by shooting himself in the head? Most likely. But the official story stipulates that Booth was shot by a Sergeant Boston Corbett. There is, however, a small problem of a ballistic nature. The bullet that killed Booth came from a pistol. Not a rifle. And it's a rifle that Sergeant Corbett had in his hands.

[38]

LAUREL

Laurel and Hardy appeared in 106 films together. Leonard and I watched about ten of them. Hardy died first. No surprise there. He was, after all, the fat one. He died amidst total indifference. Laurel was inconsolable. He died seven years later. What I'm left with? Horror. Laurel caused catastrophes. Hardy put up with them. It made people laugh. But I had lost all desire to laugh. I suddenly understood why Mark Killman had chosen us, Leonard and me. I understood what he had seen in us: A couple ruled by suffering. And I understood this so completely that I could no longer lie to myself: I was in love with Leonard. And I was suffering from this love.

[39]

ABRAHAM LINCOLN

Why erase from history the last thing John Wilkes Booth evidently accomplished: To shoot himself in the head? Why did the government of the United States find it more appropriate that the President's assassin be shot by a eunuch? Because when Boston Corbett—according to the official version—pulled the trigger of his rifle, he had no balls in his Sergeant's pants. This religious fanatic settled the question a few years earlier. To punish himself for approaching prostitutes on the street, he grabs a pair of scissors and cuts off his testicles. Liberated from these two pieces of flesh that were contaminating his soul, he goes to a prayer meeting, eats a good meal, takes a walk to aid his digestion and, finally, goes to his doctor who sews up his scrotum. Lying in bed, awakened by my nightmares, I kept looking for the answer to the following question: Why does every national tragedy turn into a miserable story about balls?

[40]

LAUREL
Scott said: "One sentence is very important to me. The one Mark said before he died."

HARDY
Chris asked: "Which one?"

ABRAHAM LINCOLN
The one you repeated to me.

LAUREL
Ah! That one!

ABRAHAM LINCOLN
Is there more than one?

HARDY
No.

ABRAHAM LINCOLN
He did say before he died: "John Wilkes Booth killed
Abraham Lincoln because he was an actor?"

LAUREL
Absolutely.

HARDY
It's possible.

LAUREL
That's what he said.

HARDY
He said so many things.

ABRAHAM LINCOLN
But he did say it?

HARDY
What?

ABRAHAM LINCOLN
That sentence.

LAUREL & HARDY
He said it. Maybe not in those words, but he said it.

ABRAHAM LINCOLN
OK. Let's say he said it in those words. Well, I think I
understand what it means. More precisely, I think I
know what Mark meant when he said that sentence. He
meant that Booth didn't kill Lincoln for political
reasons. He killed him because he was an actor.

HARDY
That's what Mark said before he died.

LAUREL
I agree with you.

ABRAHAM LINCOLN
Yes, but we need to explore the meaning of that
sentence. Booth wasn't against the abolition of slavery.
Booth supported the values of the South, it's true, but
he never would have bought a slave. What I mean is …

LAUREL & HARDY
Yes?

ABRAHAM LINCOLN
What I mean is: Booth killed the President of the United
States to make theatre. There.

LAUREL & HARDY
And …?

ABRAHAM LINCOLN
He wanted to write a page of history. To become
immortal. You understand?

LAUREL & HARDY
…

ABRAHAM LINCOLN
John Wilkes Booth is the first American star. The actor
kidnapped reality to transform it into theatre.

LAUREL
I said: "Was John Wilkes Booth in love with Abraham
Lincoln?"

HARDY
Scott said: "Good question. We can only imagine.
That's all."

HARDY
> My name is Jon Lozano. I love challenges. When Scott Johnson contacted me to be in his show, I said yes before he had time to explain the role. I'm Aries, the Ram. It's my nature to charge ahead. And Aries is the actors' sign.

LAUREL
> I'm Virgo. I scratch my head before I say yes. That's a figure of speech.

HARDY
> Introduce yourself.

LAUREL
> Yes. My name is Stewart Ozouf. I'm playing the role of Chris Levine. At first, I felt funny about playing someone I knew. We don't usually do that in the theatre. I met Chris at theatre school. We were in the same class. I worked with him a few times. In the theatre but also on TV. So when Scott asked me to play him in this show, I … I had a moment of hesitation. I thought about the implications.

HARDY
> I know what you mean. I had the same reaction when Scott told me I would play Leonard Brannigan.

LAUREL
> Your Ram put on the brakes.

HARDY
> If you want to put it that way.

LAUREL
> I'm not trying to put it any way.

HARDY
What do you mean?

LAUREL
Nothing. I'm talking nonsense. Keep going.

HARDY
Yes. I was saying that Scott asked me to play Leonard.
Given the circumstances, it wasn't easy to accept. I
asked myself if we had the right to do that. What Scott
wanted to do. Did we have the right?

LAUREL
We decided we did.

HARDY
Scott convinced us. He said it would be a way to pay
tribute to them. That life had to go on.

LAUREL
That theatre would take over life.

HARDY
But I have to admit, I was a little scared. Given the
circumstances.

LAUREL
Given the circumstances.

[42]

LAUREL
Al Pacino! I couldn't believe it. I had read in the paper
that Leonard was going to star with Al Pacino! I
wanted to kill him. Not Pacino but that asshole
Leonard! He hadn't said a thing. We saw each other
every day but he hadn't made the slightest allusion to a

film in which he was going to star with Al Pacino! Al
Pacino! I wanted to die. Al Pacino! Bastard! Bastard!

HARDY
I wanted to be sure, don't you understand? I was
waiting for everything to be signed. You should see the
contract. It's at least thirty pages. With clauses written
in Lilliputian characters.

LAUREL
Go to hell with your Lilliputian characters!

HARDY
How does it concern you anyway? I don't owe you
anything. I have my life, you have yours.

LAUREL
I would have appreciated being informed.

HARDY
You wanted to find out before everybody else? Why?

LAUREL
Because ...

HARDY
Because why? Because we worked together on a
popular TV series? Because the public imagines we're
inseparable? The public wants us to sleep together
perhaps? Is that what you think? What do you want,
Chris? What do you want from me?

[43]

ABRAHAM LINCOLN
Mark Killman Goes to the Theatre. I was stupid. I
wanted our show to open on Good Friday in a house

full of theatre people and journalists. I thought it would add spark to the performance. But what does Good Friday mean today? I was pathetic. I wanted to subtly create a parallel with April 14, 1865, another Good Friday. But really, what was I hoping that would achieve? More magic? More tragedy? As if the death of Christ belonged to me. Served me right. The bullet intended for me changed trajectory. It ended up in Leonard's chest. His chest. Too broad a word. The autopsy revealed the bullet lodged itself in the left part of his heart. What was that bullet doing there? Was it part of the show? That must have been what everyone in the audience was thinking before we heard Chris shout: "Thus ever to bastards!" The strange force with which he said that line split the show in two. In that moment, everyone realized the bullet wasn't a theatrical artifice. Chris collapsed over Leonard. He was weeping like a child. I thought about Laura Keene and I started to scream, scream, scream.

[44]

LAUREL

It took a lot of courage. I went to see Chris in prison. I wanted to know. I wanted to hear it from him. Two years had passed. In a few months, we were going to present *Laurel and Hardy Go to the Theatre*. Scott had suggested this title. He had rewritten the whole story but everyone knew what the new story was about and especially who it was about. Why had Chris Levine assassinated Leonard Brannigan? Why, instead of shooting Abraham Lincoln's wax figure with a prop gun, had he, at the last moment, pointed a real gun at Leonard? Why did Laurel kill Hardy? Basically, why does every tragedy turn into a banal story about balls?

It was Scott who was formulating these questions to help us—Jon and me—better understand our characters. In the end, we wanted to bang our heads against the wall. Scott even more than us. So I decided to go see Chris in prison. Once I found myself in front of him, I was very nervous. He looked calm. I had imagined him thinner. On the contrary, he had gained weight. He spoke slowly. I suspected he was pumped full of tranquilizers.

—Chris, do you know what we're doing?
—Yes, I know. No problem.
—I'm the one who's—
—Yes, who's going to play me. I'm happy it's you. You're a good actor, Stewart. I hope I'll be a good character.
—You're not a character.
—I am now. My life is over.
—What's the matter?
—I'm crying. It happens a lot. It's the only thing that makes me feel good. Sometimes, I even manage to forget why I'm crying. But to do that, I have to cry for a very long time. As if I were actually crying my eyes out. Along with all the images in them.
—Why did you do it?
—I don't remember.
—Were you in love with Leonard?
—If I had been in love with him, I wouldn't have killed him. Don't you think?
—I don't know.
—It's Al Pacino's fault.

HARDY
   He said: "The show has nothing to do with facts. We're
   not going to present the truth. We're going to question
   the workings of the truth."

LAUREL
   It was clear Mark Killman's ideas had contaminated
   Scott. As rehearsals went on, Scott's personality seemed
   to be changing.

HARDY
   He was becoming irritating, aggressive. He was boring
   us to tears with long speeches that meant nothing. I had
   never worked with Killman but I knew his reputation
   and I was convinced Scott was trying to be him.

LAUREL
   But he didn't have his genius. Definitely not.

ABRAHAM LINCOLN
   OK. Let's do the scene again. Because your work makes
   me want to go to the bathroom. Jon and Stewart—my
   dear Jon and Stewart—you're not hosting a daily show.
   Remove those apes' smiles from your faces. To play
   Laurel and Hardy, you have to bleed. It's the pain that
   makes them speak. Blood is always suspect. Understand?

LAUREL & HARDY
   Yes, Scott. Blood is always suspect.

ABRAHAM LINCOLN
   And why is that?

LAUREL & HARDY
   Because it's always about to be shed.

ABRAHAM LINCOLN
Case closed.

[46]

ABRAHAM LINCOLN
Since I had started working on *Laurel and Hardy Go to
the Theatre*, I felt I had finally figured out how to direct
actors. My only problem was a moral one: How far can
art go? I knew why Chris had killed Leonard. But I
didn't want to address that in my show. I wanted to go
further. I wanted to turn the assassination into art, not
into a tiresome and, in the end, banal love story. I had
overheard a conversation between Leonard and Chris
shortly before the fatal event. I had gone out to get
coffee and when I got back, I heard them talking. I
thought they were talking about me. I leaned against
the door, my coffee in my hand. Chris was calling
Leonard a bastard.

LAUREL
Bastard! Bastard!

HARDY
I wanted to be sure, don't you understand? I was
waiting for everything to be signed. You should see the
contract. It's at least thirty pages. With clauses written
in Lilliputian characters.

LAUREL
Go to hell with your Lilliputian characters!

HARDY
How does it concern you anyway? I don't owe you
anything. I have my life, you have yours.

LAUREL
I would have appreciated being informed.

HARDY
You wanted to find out before everybody else? Why?

LAUREL
Because …

HARDY
Because why? Because we worked together on a
popular TV series? Because the public imagines we're
inseparable? The public wants us to sleep together
perhaps? Is that what you think? What do you want,
Chris? What do you want from me?

LAUREL
I spoke to our agent yesterday.

HARDY
Sophie?

LAUREL
Yes.

HARDY
Well. OK. I intended to talk to you about it. After
rehearsal.

LAUREL
Well, don't waste your breath. Sophie already told me
they're shooting another season of *Case Unclosed*.
Twelve new episodes.

HARDY
Exactly. I wanted to—

LAUREL
Sophie also told me she got in touch with you and you—

HARDY
Listen, Chris. I don't want you to think—

LAUREL
And you told her that doing the series with me was out of the question and that—

HARDY
I didn't say that. Sophie must have misinterpreted what—

LAUREL
Sophie understood you very well. You even suggested names for a replacement. What kind of heart do you have in there? I've become that mediocre to you? I could tarnish your reputation, perhaps?

HARDY
Listen to me. I explained to Sophie that my shooting schedule for the film with Al Pacino created a problem and that we first needed—

LAUREL
Al Pacino! Yes, of course. Al Pacino! Of course. When one stars with Al Pacino, one can't afford to appear with Chris Levine.

HARDY
You don't understand. I can't …

LAUREL
Can't …?

HARDY
Chris, it would be better if we didn't work together anymore. After this show, I want us to—

LAUREL
You want to erase me from your life.

HARDY
I just want to—

ABRAHAM LINCOLN
I didn't want to hear any more. I thought rehearsals would become hell. I went to the bathroom and waited a good fifteen minutes. My stomach was hurting. I gathered my courage and went back to work. I opened the door slowly. Chris and Leonard were rehearsing as if nothing had happened. But I knew nothing was the same anymore.

[47]

ABRAHAM LINCOLN
We're now going to work the end of the show. Here's how I see it. You'll see, it's kind of experimental. No, I shouldn't use that word. It's kind of ... how can I say ... poetic? No. Kind of ...

LAUREL
Metaphorical?

ABRAHAM LINCOLN
In a way but—

HARDY
If you want my opinion, words can't describe what we're doing.

ABRAHAM LINCOLN
You're right, Jon. You just expressed very clearly what I was—

LAUREL
Blah blah blah. Can we get started with the end?

ABRAHAM LINCOLN
The end. Yes. Very important in a show. OK, the idea came to me after Mark Killman's death. Quickly, here's how the last scene should play. Just before shooting Lincoln, John Wilkes Booth points his gun at Harry Hawk ...

LAUREL & HARDY
Harry Hawk?

ABRAHAM LINCOLN
Harry Hawk, the actor who was playing the American cousin in question. You remember, don't you? Asa Trenchard?

HARDY
But why would Booth want to kill him?

LAUREL
Why not Laura Keene? It would be even more spectacular. He kills his lover before killing the President. Not bad, huh?

ABRAHAM LINCOLN
Because it's not Florence Trenchard who's alone on stage at the time of Lincoln's assassination. It's Asa Trenchard. And I want to be faithful to at least that part of the story. No, it's a lot more interesting if Booth kills Harry Hawk. He was a good-looking actor— young and promising. It's perfectly natural to believe he

had an affair with Laura Keene. In killing him, Booth gets rid of a rival.

LAUREL
He kills two birds with one stone.

ABRAHAM LINCOLN
So, Booth kills Harry Hawk, then puts a bullet in Lincoln's head, then, *coup de théâtre*, leaps from the presidential box onto the stage, shouts his "*Sic semper tyrannis*" and ... shoots himself in the head in front of a confused and admiring audience in a state of aesthetic shock.

LAUREL
And we hear Laura Keene scream, scream, scream in her enormous skirt that's swallowing her future.

ABRAHAM LINCOLN
Not at all. At that moment, hovering between life and death, a bullet behind his right eye, Abraham Lincoln painfully gets up and raises an arm. The audience goes silent and holds its breath. Abraham Lincoln starts to dance. He dances his life, he dances his death, he dances America. He's a wax figure—cracking, splitting, crumbling and coming apart. And you know to what music? *Madama Butterfly*!

[48]

HARDY
Scott Johnson had lost his mind. The show was turning into a gong show. Who was going to recognize, in this mess he was making us rehearse, dressed like Laurel and Hardy, a tribute to painful events? A tribute to men who had really lived?

LAUREL

Like me, you had a bad feeling, right? Jon, I'm talking
to you!

HARDY

I'm sorry, Stewart. My mind was elsewhere.

LAUREL

I was asking if you too had a—

HARDY

—bad feeling. Yes. A very bad feeling. To be honest, I
dreaded another tragic event. Scott insisted he knew the
truth about Mark's death. Mark hadn't died from an
aggressive cancer. As the media had claimed.

LAUREL

Scott was ranting. He wanted to convince us that Mark
had premeditated his death. He kept saying that Mark
created his show *John Wilkes Booth Goes to the
Theatre* in order to commit suicide. To turn his suicide
into a show.

HARDY

He had poisoned himself slowly, day after day, during
rehearsals.

LAUREL

Scott, in his madness, believed Mark wanted to die on
stage, on opening night, in his wax costume, as
Abraham Lincoln's figure, while dancing the death of
America!

LAUREL & HARDY

The death of America.

HARDY

But the poison had worked more quickly than expected.
Mark died in the middle of rehearsal.

LAUREL
That's what Scott had gotten into his head after
rereading and rewriting Mark Killman's notebook to
death.

HARDY
That's why we had a bad feeling.

[49]

ABRAHAM LINCOLN
One sentence in Mark Killman's notebook intrigued
me. He had written: "Turn the figure into a geisha." I
had a feeling the key to his show was hiding in these
two words: Figure and geisha. Suddenly, I was hit by a
bolt of lightning. It all became clear. Figure, geisha,
Lincoln. Yes. Of course. It was obvious. Mark Killman
was thinking about Madama Butterfly. A geisha who's
passionately in love with an American. Not an
American cousin. Not an Asa Trenchard. But a Yankee,
nothing less. What was his name again?

He hums a few notes from Madama Butterfly.

Pinkerton! Madama Butterfly commits suicide for the
love of Benjamin Franklin Pinkerton! A man who
humiliated her, abandoned her. A man who showed
contempt for her ancestors. The pinnacle of opera. A
tragic number. And a grotesque farce. I have the end of
my show. The bullet from the Deringer goes through
my skull. I collapse. I vomit blood. Then I get up. I'm a
crumbling wax figure. A dying President. An Apollo in
flames. I dance to the music of a kimono who's
committing *hara-kiri* for America. That's it, I found
the end!

LAUREL
In the last act, Madama Butterfly watches, through a spyglass, the arrival of the American ship that's bringing Benjamin Franklin Pinkerton back to Japan after a three-year absence. He's coming back with a new wife on his arm. A real one this time. An American. Not a cheap Japanese doll.

HARDY
The ship's name is *Abraham Lincoln*. A detail.

LAUREL
But Scott is convinced that this trivial detail gives him the right to end the show with Puccini.

HARDY
I hate opera. Go get it.

LAUREL
It's time?

HARDY
It's time. Go get it.

LAUREL
I would like to say something first.

HARDY
Is it in the script?

LAUREL
How would we know?

HARDY
By saying it. So?

LAUREL
No. Nothing. I don't know what I wanted to say.

HARDY
Then go get it.

LAUREL
I'm going.

> *LAUREL exits the stage. He comes back with a wax figure of ABRAHAM LINCOLN.*

HARDY
Be careful!

LAUREL
It's not that fragile.

HARDY
There's the beginning of a crack around the nose.

LAUREL
So what, a crack around the nose?

HARDY
That's how it always starts.

LAUREL
What?

HARDY
After the nose, the eyes; after the eyes, the mouth—

ABRAHAM LINCOLN
OK, OK, we get it! No need to repeat everything! Let's go right to the end. Here, take this.

> *He gives LAUREL a gun.*

Now. Asa Trenchard steps toward the audience and delivers his famous line. At the same time, John Wilkes Booth sneaks into the presidential box, a Deringer in his hand. Take your place! Come on! What are you waiting for? Start the scene!

HARDY
Don't know the manners of good society, eh? Well, I guess I know enough to turn you inside out, old gal— you sockdologizing old man-trap!

ABRAHAM LINCOLN
What are you waiting for? Kill him!

LAUREL
I ...

ABRAHAM LINCOLN
Shoot! Point and shoot! You hate him. He's a rival. An amateur who slept with Laura, the great Laura Keene. Harry Hawk is a bad actor who wants to take your place. Why not get rid of him before committing the crime that will make you eternal? Killing an actor before killing a U.S. President is trivial, it's true. But it's unique. So you kill him, you kill me and you kill yourself. Have you ever heard of an easier scene to play?

LAUREL
No. I don't think so.

ABRAHAM LINCOLN
Good.

HARDY
Do I say my line again?

ABRAHAM LINCOLN
Shut up. Yes, say it again. And don't forget—once you're dead, you don't move! I don't even want to hear

you breathe. I, over here, have a dance to do. I don't
want any interference.

HARDY
Don't know the manners of good society, eh? Well ...
well ... well, I guess I know enough to turn you inside
out, old gal—you sockdologizing old man-trap!

*LAUREL kills HARDY. Then he shoots
ABRAHAM LINCOLN.*

LAUREL
Thus ever to bastards!

*LAUREL kills himself. Silence. We hear Madame
Butterfly, the aria "Un Bel Di Vedremo."
Abraham Lincoln's wax figure gets up and
dances, dances, dances the death of America.*

End.

Translator's Acknowledgements

Thank you to the actors and directors who participated in the early development of this translation: David Beazely, Matt Boston, Elizabeth Diamond, Brian Dykstra, Patrick Frederic, Trevor Leigh, Margarett Perry, Paul Rainville, Kurt Rhodes and David Wilson Barnes. And a very special thank you to the entire staff of the Lark Play Development Center and Alberta Theatre Projects.